SWEET PAPER CRAFTS

SWEET PAPER CRAFTS

25 Simple Projects to Brighten Your Life

MOLLIE GREENE

Photographs by J. Aaron Greene

CHRONICLE BOOKS

SAN FRANCISCO

Library of Congress Cataloging-in-Publication Data:
Greene, Mollie.
  Sweet paper crafts ; 25 simple projects to brighten your life /
by Mollie Greene ; photographs by J. Aaron Greene.
    pages cm
  ISBN 978-1-4521-1680-8 (pbk.)
1. Paper work. I. Title.

  TT870.G73 2013
  745.54–dc23

                        2012030763

Manufactured in China

MIX
Paper from
responsible sources
FSC® C008047
www.fsc.org

Designed by Jennifer Tolo Pierce

Dritz Fray Check is a registered trademark of General Dispersions
Inc. Etsy is a registered trademark of Etsy, Inc. Goo Gone is a registered
trademark of Magic American Products, Inc. Mod Podge is a registered
trademark of Enterprise Paint Manufacturing Corp. Scotch Wrinkle-
free Glue Stick is a registered trademark of 3M Corp. X-ACTO knife is a
registered trademark of Elmer's Products, Inc. Yes! Paste is a registered
trademark of Gane Brothers & Lane.

10 9 8 7 6 5 4 3 2 1

Chronicle Books LLC
680 Second Street
San Francisco, California 94107
www.chroniclebooks.com

For my little Dot

CONTENTS

▽ ▽ ▽ ▽ ▽ ▽ ▽

INTRODUCTION

▼ ▼ ▼ ▼ ▼

With just minimal tools and supplies anyone can make unique paper finery. Creating simple gift tags and paper flowers, lengths of garlands, fluttering chandeliers, and mobiles that turn with a breeze—all from paper and other basic materials—is a satisfying way to work with your hands and fashion something lovely in the process.

I've collected paper scraps, unusual buttons, and bits of ribbon since I was a child, always inspired by the notion that something new could be crafted from a collection of old things. Turning my lifetime love of making things into my daily work was a natural progression. One day in 2008, on a whim, I began selling paper garlands and gift packaging in my Etsy store, Royal Buffet. To my surprise, the shop took off, and soon my nights and weekends were spent clipping paper butterflies for wreaths and measuring shiny thread for mobiles. Over time, more and more people asked about the process behind my creations. In this book, you'll find the techniques that I've been able to perfect over the years. Making beautiful things with my hands has brought me a great deal of satisfaction and happiness, and I hope that the projects in this book bring the same to you.

In *Sweet Paper Crafts* you will learn the tools and techniques needed to craft stunning paper creations for all occasions. I love to work with found, recycled papers because of the variety of interesting images, textures, colors, and typography. Combining these elements makes each project exciting to work on and the results distinctive. You'll see a variety of found papers used in the following pages, such as record jackets, book pages, crepe paper, and tissue paper. I also love working with glitter and ribbon. The twenty-five projects range from simple Butterfly Shimmer Tags, Prancing Reindeer Ornaments, and Galloping Cupcake Toppers to intricate mobiles, like the Alice in Wonderland Mobile, and papier-mâché sculptures like the Gentle Rabbit Taxidermy.

Whether you are a beginner or an expert crafter, I hope you will be inspired to create something beautiful out of the humblest pieces of paper. So clear off your desk, grab your scissors, and let's make something together!

MATERIALS, TOOLS, *and* TIPS

PAPER

Whether discovered at a thrift store book bin or acquired new from an art supply store, paper for crafty projects is easy to come by and inexpensive to collect. Here are some tips for sourcing paper and creating your own stash.

Books, Maps, Magazines, and Newspapers

I find that repurposed paper from old books, maps, and magazines is ideal for many paper projects. Recycling vintage books is economical and eco-friendly, and also makes each piece you create one of a kind. A treasure trove of interesting paper can be found at thrift shops and yard sales and possibly in your own basement or attic. Faded botanical prints, text in foreign languages, and tissue-paper-thin pages from old dictionaries are fun to work with and give finished pieces a vintage charm.

When considering used books, feel the pages individually and then in layers. If the paper is brittle and won't fold without cracking, it won't work well. You should be able to make a strong crease when you fold the page. Next, smell the paper. Nothing is worse than creating a project with pages that smell like an ashtray! Old-book smell is fine and usually fades after the pages are aired out, but avoid the odor of cigarette smoke, mildew, and mothballs when choosing used materials.

Old dictionaries have thin, sturdy paper that is easy to work with. Vintage children's books often have wonderful colors and textures, and many have been damaged by a wayward crayon or marker,

which makes for a clear conscience when you snip away at the pages. I prefer older magazines to new ones, as the paper tends to be thicker and shinier.

Newspaper works well for stuffing paper sculptures—as for the Gentle Rabbit Taxidermy (page 115) and Percher Bird (page 23). I always use newspaper to protect my work surface from things like glue and polyurethane and to ease in cleaning up any glitter mess.

Record Jackets and Cardboard

Many records that flood the shelves of thrift stores aren't worth a listen. But the jackets have beautiful typography and colors, making them a great material for several projects in this book, such as gift tags, mobiles, and package toppers. Choose sturdy jackets free of stains and stickers. When you bring them home, you can toss the vinyl (or think of something to make with it!), but check the inner paper liner to see if it's suitable for future use.

Lightweight cardboard such as cereal and cracker boxes come in handy as well. It can be fun to come up with fresh uses for paper towel tubes, as I did for the Party Popper (page 73). Stash a few tubes and boxes away to use when the inspiration hits.

Store-bought Paper

When buying new paper from an art supply or craft store, first stock up on the basics. I recommend having artist sketch paper, tracing paper, bristol board, and card stock on hand. Specialty papers like scrapbooking paper, tissue paper, honeycomb paper, butcher paper, and origami paper are easily available in craft stores or online when a project calls for them. I find that it's more cost-effective to buy specialty papers on a project-to-project basis. Over time you'll accumulate a nice collection of loose pages and scraps for future projects.

For the flowers in the Flower Fancy Wreath (page 65) and for trims and fringe on other projects, you will need crepe paper folds in a variety of colors. If you enjoy making these projects, you may want to store a generous supply. When working with fine papers like tissue and crepe, purchase a high-quality variety in order to keep tearing at a minimum. Sewing patterns found in the craft section of thrift stores (or at craft and fabric stores) are made of a fine tissue paper in a nice neutral brown or gray. This tissue paper can be used interchangeably with standard tissue paper, although be sure to check for quality and only use sewing pattern tissue that does not tear at the slightest fold. We'll use sewing pattern tissue in the Flowering Chandelier (page 47).

Embossed gold die cuts are a good choice for special lettering. Beautiful embellished letters of the alphabet come in a variety of typographies and are fun to attach to cards and tags using glue or thread. Feathers, hearts, and other die-cut shapes are also available at most specialty craft stores.

Sandpaper is needed when preparing surfaces to decorate with paper. A standard medium-grade sandpaper will work well for most decoupage projects.

PAPER TOOLS

A bone folder is a tool with a dull edge used to score paper to create a clean fold. It's very handy for making a Pretty People Card and Envelope (page 53) and for scoring the binding fold on a Scratch Book (page 35).

A slotted quilling tool is a small device for making tight spiral curls out of paper strips. It has a little groove in the top in which you insert one end of a strip of paper before wrapping the entire strip around the tip. The tool is needed for the Blooming Brooch (page 18).

A wide range of paper punches can be found in most craft stores, but, as with paper, it's best to stick to the basics. By using classic punch shapes and creating your own templates for more complicated shapes (see page 16), you will save money and make your work more distinctive. Classic punch shapes to keep on hand include circles in a variety of diameters, stars, squares, triangles, teardrops, flowers, and tags. A small star punch, for instance, is used for the Tiny Star Garland (page 33). To save time when making confetti, I like to use a multiple-hole punch as directed in the Galloping Cupcake Toppers (page 120). Medallion-edge punches can be hard to come by, but you can get a similar result by cutting out a circle with a decorative-edge scissors.

A ruler or a measuring tape is necessary for measuring paper and ribbon to the correct length. I prefer a wooden or plastic ruler to a measuring tape because it stays in place while marking paper, but either will do.

An iron is sometimes needed to press out creases in paper. Tissue paper and sewing pattern tissue work best when they are wrinkle free, and an iron with a low, no-steam setting will safely smooth the paper so it's ready to cut.

SCISSORS

Fancy scissors are not required for the projects in this book. You will need two pairs of new craft scissors with sharp blades and good grips. Reserve one pair for cutting paper and card stock and the other for cutting stiff materials like bristol board, paper tubing, record jackets, and cereal boxes. Scissors used to cut stiff materials will dull faster and can ruin fine papers. You will also want a small pair of scissors for detail clipping.

An X-ACTO knife is good for cutting areas that are too small for a pair of scissors. Pinking shears, scallop scissors, and fringe scissors are for cutting fun edges or extra detail. A paper cutter makes quick, clean, measured cuts and is required for a few projects in this book. Wire cutters are essential for cutting wire, as scissors used to cut wire will be ruined.

ADHESIVES AND FINISHES

Look for products labeled "acid free," "wrinkle free," and "dries clear." Stock up on a standard, inexpensive liquid glue like Tacky Glue. It is used for many projects in this book because it is strong and versatile, and dries clear. You will also need glue sticks that prevent wrinkles, since Tacky Glue will cause paper to wrinkle and warp if you use too much or use it on a thin paper like crepe or tissue paper. I recommend a good-quality glue stick like Scotch Wrinkle-free Glue Stick because it is easy to control and lasts through many projects.

Thin liquid glues like Mod Podge are useful for covering large areas with glitter and are needed for finishing off paper sculptures and decoupage projects. Use a foam brush to apply Mod Podge for the best results.

Yes! Paste is a very thick, sticky glue that helps keep objects upright. A hot glue gun comes in handy for adhering paper flowers to brooch pins, as in the Blooming Brooch (page 18), or for heavy, large-scale projects.

Sweet Paper Crafts

Polyurethane, a plastic material in liquid form, brings a nice finished look to collage projects, like the Striped Decoupage Picture Frame (page 69). Apply polyurethane with a foam brush as you would Mod Podge. Polyurethane comes in several gloss levels; choose the type based on how shiny you want your finished piece to look.

A foam brush is necessary for applying Mod Podge or polyurethane. Foam brushes come in a variety of sizes and are inexpensive, easy to clean, and easy to replace. Use smaller brushes for applying Mod Podge to pieces with lots of crevices and larger brushes for wider areas.

Applying a small amount of liquid fray preventive like Dritz Fray Check to the ends of ribbons or threads will keep them from shedding or fraying. Use a fray preventive on the thread ends of garlands that you plan on hanging outdoors repeatedly.

A glue remover such as Goo Gone is helpful for cleaning off stickers, old glue, or any other coating on the frame for the Striped Decoupage Picture Frame (page 69) or on the lampshade for the Flowering Chandelier (page 47).

A variety of tapes are essential for paper projects. Masking tape is used to create the structure for the Gentle Rabbit Taxidermy (page 115) and other papier-mâché projects. Double-sided tape is good for attaching items like the Paper Ship Package Topper (page 101) to gifts. Floral tape finishes off the paper flowers adorning the Flower Fancy Wreath (page 65). Japanese washi tape is a fun decorative tape for packaging and cards. Circle stickers or medallion stickers (a circle with a scalloped or pinked edge) are for sealing envelopes and decorating packaging.

THREAD AND STRING

Gather threads of all colors as you find them at thrift stores and flea markets. Old threads can break easily, so test them before you make lengths of garland. Keep a supply of colors that you like and include some metallic thread for projects like the Flowering Chandelier (page 47). Embroidery floss and string work well for tags, ornaments, and long garlands. You will also want to have ribbon, yarn, clear monofilament, and baker's twine in your stash. The type of thread or string you use will depend on the style you're after.

WIRE

You'll need heavy-gauge wire, sold in hardware stores, for making wreaths. Other projects require different types of thin wire. Cloth-wrapped floral wire (available in several colors), fine silver wire (on a spool), and straight stick floral wire are available in the floral section of craft stores. Be sure to use wire cutters, not scissors, to cut wire!

GLITTER

Craft glitter is available in many colors, shapes, and qualities. A standard-size glitter is used for projects like the mini top hat (see page 83). Fine dusting glitter is harder to control than standard-size glitter, so experimentation from project to project is best. German glass glitter is pricey, but can take an ornament from pretty to brilliant, so consider keeping it in stock for special projects or to use in small amounts, like on the Prancing Reindeer Ornaments (page 77).

MAKING TEMPLATES

I've created templates for many projects in the book to help you cut out the required pieces. You can easily download the templates at www.chroniclebooks.com/sweetpaper. You can also make your own templates, even if you do not feel confident drawing figures by hand. A simple way to create a template is to find a shape you like in a book or magazine. Cut out the shape and make a copy of it to enlarge or shrink the image. When you get it to the size you like, cut it out—and you have a template! To transfer your template to sturdier paper or cardboard, trace around your shape and cut it out.

ORGANIZATION

Being organized minimizes frustrations and helps you keep track of small pieces you've cut and find the right tools when you need them. Here are some of my tried-and-true tips.

✳ Work over a tray with a rim to catch all your clippings as you go— this makes cleanup a breeze.

✳ Use bowls, cups, or other small dishes to hold the components of your projects so you can easily find them when you need them.

✳ A clothespin tied to a string that is looped around a ceiling hook will give you an easy, hand-level way to hang your mobiles and chandeliers while you work on them.

✳ Store templates in labeled envelopes or drawers, and put the templates, especially small ones, away immediately after use.

✳ Tape a label on your scissors so you know which one is for fine paper and which one is for stiff paper.

✳ Keep moist wipes at the ready to clean any excess glue off your work surface or your hands.

✳ Completely clear off your work space after you finish a project so that you can start in on the next project without having to clean up first.

✳ Last, but certainly not least, walk away from a project when you feel frustrated. This will give you perspective and prevent you from giving up entirely.

Sweet Paper Crafts

PROJECTS

BLOOMING BROOCH

These lovely blooms are pretty pinned on a lapel, the brim of a hat, or the first sundress of the season. And besides, a flower that refuses to wilt is nothing to sniff at. You can alter the templates to make a large single bloom if you like. Brooch pins can be found at your local craft store.

Supplies

Blooming Brooch templates

Pencil

Book pages

Scissors for paper

Slotted quilling tool

Liquid glue

Ruler

Tissue paper

Toothpick

Crepe paper

Record jacket front or back

Scissors for cardboard

Brooch pin

Hot glue gun and hot glue sticks

Circle or medallion punch

Scrap paper

Glue stick

1. Download the Blooming Brooch templates at www.chroniclebooks.com/sweetpaper. Using the pencil, trace the three flower circle templates on the book pages. Cut out the circles with the paper scissors. Be careful to cut inside the pencil lines so that you don't have to erase them later. Cut each circle into a spiral, beginning at the perimeter and ending with a round area in the center.

2. Attach the outer end of the paper spiral to the slit of the quilling tool and begin wrapping the spiral around the tool. When you reach the rounded center of the spiral, gently remove the paper from the quilling tool and let it spin out to form a loose coil. Place the round center on a flat surface and allow the coil to form a loose flower shape. Apply a small amount of liquid glue to several points in the coil to hold it in place. Repeat with the remaining two spirals. You now have three flower coils.

3. To make stamens for the flowers, cut three 1½ -in/4-cm squares of tissue paper. Fold each square lengthwise into fourths. Hold the top of the folded paper in one hand and make closely spaced parallel cuts into the other end, cutting about three-fourths of the way, to make fringe. Twist the top of the fringe to make a pointed end. Apply

{continued}

Sweet Paper Crafts

a dot of liquid glue to this "foot" and, using the toothpick, press the end of the stamen into the center of the flower coil. The fringe should fill the flower coil. Check the length. Each stamen should be level with the top of the coil or protrude no more than 1/4 to 1/2 in/6 to 12 mm. Trim the fringe if necessary. Repeat to make stamens for the remaining two flowers.

4. To embellish your flowers, make a tassel of crepe paper that will sit underneath the flowers and peek out from the brooch. Cut a 3-by-5-in/7.5-by-12-cm piece of crepe paper and fold lengthwise into fourths. Cut the paper for the tassel in the same way that you cut the paper for the stamens. Unfold the paper to reveal a fringe. At the top of the fringe, pinch the paper so that the uncut edge at the top gathers together. After gathering it all the way across, twist the top slightly to create a small tassel.

5. Using the pencil, trace the base template on the record jacket and cut out with cardboard scissors. Decide how you want to arrange the flowers and tassel on the base and then attach with liquid glue. Allow to dry thoroughly, about an hour.

6. Attach the base to the brooch pin using the hot glue gun. Allow to dry for about 10 minutes. Punch one or two circles out of the scrap paper. Using the glue stick, apply glue to a circle and place it on the top of the glued-down pin end to finish the backside of the brooch. Trim the fringe on the tassel if you like.

Sweet Paper Crafts

STEP 1 //////////////////////////// STEP 2 //

STEP 3 ///

//////////////////////////// STEP 4 //////////////////////////// STEP 5 ////////////////////////////

//////////////////////////// STEP 6 //

{*continued*}

Blooming Brooch

Sweet Paper Crafts

PERCHER BIRD

▼▼▼▼▼▼▼

Let a flock of these little birds alight around your house for cheerful company and eye-catching decor. Working with papier-mâché is easy when you use the templates and instructions here. You can enlarge or reduce the templates to make chirpers of different sizes.

1. Download the Percher Bird templates at www.chroniclebooks.com/sweetpaper. Open the cereal box and lay it out flat. Using the pencil and templates, trace two bodies, two wings, one breast, and one tail feather on the box. Cut out the pieces with the cardboard scissors. Holding the two body pieces together, attach them along the head and back with a piece of masking tape. Keep applying masking tape where the bodies meet to secure pieces.

2. Slip the breast piece between the body pieces, inserting the pointed end at the head and curving the breast piece slightly so that it aligns with the bottom of the body pieces. Use masking tape to secure the breast piece along the edges where it meets the body. Stuff a little newspaper inside the body to fill out the bird and make it a bit stiffer. Tape the wings in place on either side of the body. Bend the wings a bit so that they come away from the bird. Reinforce with tape as needed to keep the wings in place. Fold the tail feather piece in half to create a crease. Tape in place at the back of the bird. Cover the entire bird with masking tape, using plenty of tape to make the bird stiff, especially in the wing and tail feather areas, but be careful to apply the tape evenly so that the bird is not front or back heavy.

{continued}

Supplies

. . . .

Percher Bird templates

Cereal box

Pencil

Scissors for cardboard

Masking tape

Newspaper

Ruler

Scrap wire

Wire cutters

20-gauge straight stick floral wire

Thin liquid glue such as Mod Podge

Small dish

Papers

2 foam brushes

Polyurethane (optional)

3. On the underside of the bird, at about the center of the bird's belly, make two marks with the pencil, each about 3/4 in/2 cm from either side of the underside of the bird. Using a piece of scrap wire, punch holes for the legs. Widen these holes with your cardboard scissors. Using the wire cutters, cut an 8-in/46-cm piece of floral wire, then cut it in half. Hold the two pieces of wire together (as if you have one piece of wire) and push them into one of the leg holes. Push the wires through the bird and out through the other leg hole. Pull until you have an equal length protruding from each hole. Bend each end to make feet about 2½ in/6 cm long. See if the bird will stand. If the legs are in the right location and the feet are big enough and the right distance apart, the bird should support itself. It may take a few tests before you get the placement right. If the bird is front or back heavy, you may need to make cuts into the belly and move the legs back or forward until the bird stands on its own. Once the bird stands, secure the legs at the entry and exit points with masking tape.

4. (I recommend spreading newspaper on your work surface before starting this step.) Pour a small amount of glue into the dish. Tear your chosen papers into strips of varying lengths and widths. Pieces 3 in/7.5 cm long are easiest to work with. One at a time, dip the pieces into the glue, covering them entirely, and then use a foam brush to wipe any excess glue into the dish. Apply the pieces in over-lapping layers all over the bird, going

{*continued*}

around and behind the wings and under the breast and tail feathers. It is important to wipe away excess glue from each piece and to use a light hand to avoid creating bumps and wrinkles in the paper. Let the bird dry standing up. The first layer should take at least an hour to dry thoroughly. Check for places that need more coverage, apply more paper as needed, and let dry again.

5. When the bird has dried and you don't need to add more layers, apply a final coat of liquid glue or, if desired, a layer of polyurethane, using a clean foam brush. Allow to dry overnight.

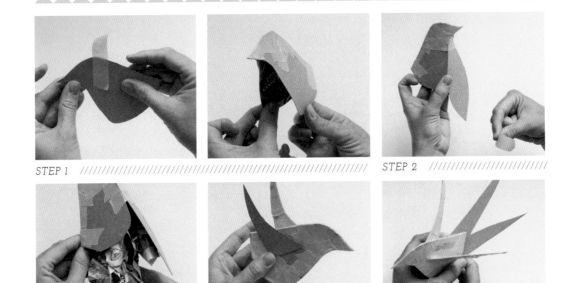

STEP 1 /// STEP 2 /////////////////////////////

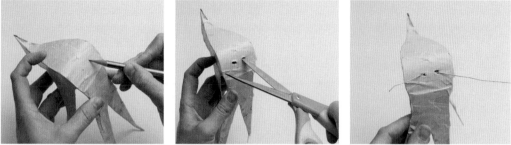

//

// ///////////////////////////

Percher Bird

27

BUTTERFLY SHIMMER TAGS

Perch these glittering butterflies atop packages, or make the tags the very gift. You can add an underlayer to the wings cut from metallic or colorful paper, or cover the entire tag with glitter when you're finished. You may want to glue a paper circle or rectangle to the back of each tag so you have a place to write a greeting. The possibilities are endless when it comes to fancy gift packaging!

1. Download the Butterfly Shimmer Tags templates from www.chroniclebooks.com/ sweetpaper. To make four tags, use the butterfly template and a pencil to trace twelve butterflies on your chosen paper. With the paper scissors, cut out the butterflies. Be careful to cut inside the pencil lines so that you don't have to erase them later. Trace four tag templates on bristol board and cut out with the cardboard scissors.

2. Punch a hole in the top of each tag with the small hole punch. Cut an 8-in/20-cm piece of string for each tag. Fold the strings in half, thread the loops through the hole in the tags, bring the ends through the loops, and pull tight. If using ribbon, you may want to apply a fine line of fray preventive across the ends to keep them tidy.

3. With the circle punch, punch four circles from paper of a contrasting color. Using the glue stick, apply glue to the circles and adhere one circle to the front of each tag, slightly above the center. Apply a small amount of liquid glue to the underside of the body of a butterfly (not to the wings) and attach it to a circle on one of the tags. Repeat to glue two more butterflies to the

{continued}

Supplies
....

Butterfly Shimmer Tags templates

Pencil

Papers

Scissors for paper

Bristol board or record jacket

Scissors for cardboard

Small hole or teardrop punch

String, yarn, twine, or ribbon

Liquid fray preventive (optional)

1-in/2.5-cm circle or medallion punch

Glue stick

Liquid glue

Scrap paper

Glitter

tag, one on top of the other. (There should be a total of three butterflies on each tag.) Repeat with the remaining tags and butterflies and allow to dry completely, about an hour. Gently bend the wings of each tag forward for a more fluttery effect.

4. Apply the tiniest bit of liquid glue to the edges of the wings of the butterflies on each tag and to a corner or two of the tags. Holding the tag over a piece of scrap paper, sprinkle glitter onto the glued edges and corners. Allow to dry thoroughly, about an hour.

STEP 1 //

STEP 2 //////////////////////////////

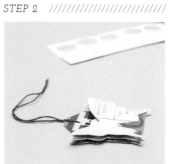

STEP 3 //

//

STEP 4 ///

Butterfly Shimmer Tags

TINY STAR GARLAND

If you have small scraps of paper just large enough to punch with tiny shapes, save them in a box for projects such as this garland. A star is just one of the cutouts you can use to make garlands to string from room to room and beyond. The sky is the limit when you consider all the punches available.

1. With the scissors, cut thread to the length of the garland you want to make. If you are using fine thread, the garland should be no longer than 6 to 10 ft/5.5 to 9 m to prevent knots and tangles. You can make additional garlands, if needed, and hang them end to end. Tie a loop in one end of your thread.

2. Using the star-shaped punch, punch out a number of stars from your chosen papers, letting them fall into the bowl.

3. Lay out about ten stars in a row away from you, placing them right-side down. Apply a small dot of liquid glue to the center of each star. (If using a star punch 1 in/2.5 cm or larger, you may want to cover the stars with glue stick and then with dots of liquid glue. This will keep the edges together when you apply another layer of stars in the next step.)

4. Beginning at the end of the thread with the loop, place the thread on the dot of glue on the star closest to you. Choose a star from the bowl and set it right-side up on the thread, aligning the points of the two stars. Repeat with the remaining stars

{*continued*}

Supplies

. . . .

Scissors

Ruler

Thread

Small star-shaped punch

Papers

Bowl or cup

Liquid glue

Glue stick (optional)

in the row, spacing them as far apart or as close together as you'd like. Continue making rows of stars, dotting them with glue, and attaching the thread and the stars from the bowl until you reach the end of your garland.

5. Tie a loop at the other end of the thread and string your garland wherever you want to add a bit of whimsy.

STEP 1 ///////////////////////// STEP 2 ///////////////////////// STEP 3 /////////////////////////

STEP 4 //

SCRATCH BOOK

Little notebooks are ideal for making lists and jotting down things you don't want to forget. This scratch book is lightweight and easy to tuck into a pocket—and when you create your own, it is one of a kind. Make a stack of books and keep them in your desk drawer or tie them together with twine and give them as a gift.

1. Using the paper cutter, cut a cover for the book from the sturdy paper. It should be 10 in by 3 1/2 in/25 by 9 cm. Fold the cover in half widthwise and score with the bone folder. Using the paper cutter again, cut five pieces of blank paper each 3 by 9 1/2 in/ 7.5 by 24 cm. Stack the five pieces and fold in half widthwise. Score the fold.

2. Center the pages inside the cover. With the scissors, cut a 10-in/25-cm piece of baker's twine. Thread the twine through the needle. Open the book to the center and use the needle to pierce holes at the top and bottom of the fold, working through both the pages and the cover. Starting at the bottom hole, push the needle through the layers, pulling the twine and leaving at least 2 in/5 cm inside the book. Bring the needle through the hole at the top. Tighten the twine and tie the ends in a small knot. Clip any excess twine. Close the book and place under a heavy book for 24 hours to completely flatten.

{*continued*}

Supplies

Paper cutter

Sturdy magazine or children's book pages

Bone folder

Blank paper

Scissors for paper

Ruler

Baker's twine

Yarn needle

Heavy book

STEP 1 ///

STEP 2 ///

///

ALICE IN WONDERLAND MOBILE

Inspiration for this mobile comes from the Cheshire Cat's wise admonition, "Depends a good deal on where you want to get to." You want to use papers that are not too flimsy so that the shapes will hang without flopping over, but not too thick so that the mobile will still have an airy, light feeling. Choose papers that coordinate in color and design and are similar weights. You may want to select pages from the same magazine article or children's book for continuity; mixing styles of paper and combining papers with text and images will also work well. The string or yarn should be able to support the weight of the mobile without breaking.

Supplies

Alice in Wonderland Mobile templates

Pencil

Sturdy magazine or book pages

Scissors for paper

Glue stick

Wire cutters

Ruler

20-gauge straight stick floral wire

Sturdy string or yarn

Liquid glue

Scrap paper

1. Download the Alice in Wonderland Mobile templates from www.chroniclebooks/sweetpaper.com. Using the pencil, trace the cat head template on your chosen paper. Trace the Cheshire smile template on paper of a contrasting color. Cut out both pieces with the paper scissors. Be careful to cut inside the pencil lines so that you don't have to erase them later. Using the glue stick, affix the smile to the cat's head.

2. Trace the kitten template on paper and cut out. Trace four stars and cut out. Fold a piece of paper and place the two pennant templates along the fold as marked, then trace and cut out. Trace each letter template on paper and cut out.

3. Using the wire cutters, cut two pieces of floral wire each 18 in/46 cm long. Using the scissors, cut a piece of string 25 in/63.5 cm long. Place the two wires together and overlap them so that the total length of the wires is 20 in/50 cm. In the center of the overlapped wires, tie one end of the string with a firm knot. Make a loop in the other end and hang the wires.

{continued}

4. Cut two pieces of string each about 18 in/ 46 cm long. Tie each piece to an end of the wires where they still overlap, leaving the string hanging down. If the wires do not hang horizontally, slide your center knot left or right.

5. Cut three lengths of string about 14 in/ 35.5 cm, 17 in/43 cm, and 18 in/46 cm long. Place the lengths of string on your work surface in three rows, with the shortest away from you and the longest close to you. Arrange the letters as follows: "DEPENDS A GOOD" on the short length, "DEAL ON WHERE" on the next, and "YOU WANT TO GET TO" on the long one. Check your spacing. The words should be readable when hung. Each length of string should have about 4 in/10 cm on either end for tying to the mobile.

6. Turn the letters right-side down, keeping them in the same order. Starting with the shortest piece of string, place a dot of liquid glue at the top of the D. Set the string in the glue and press firmly. Continue gluing the letters of the first three words, spacing them evenly and allowing space between the words. The glue will dry clear; if you do not use too much, you won't even see it on the backs of the letters. Continue to glue the remaining words on the remaining lengths of string. Allow to dry for about 15 minutes before continuing. Turn the strings of words right-side up.

7. Center "DEPENDS A GOOD" on the mobile and tie each end of the string to the wire. Tie "DEAL ON WHERE" to the mobile, making sure it hangs below the first three words. Finally, tie "YOU WANT TO GET TO" in the same way. Adjust the knots if

Sweet Paper Crafts

each part of the phrase is not centered on the wire. The words add weight, so you may have to adjust the top support string until the mobile balances.

8. Place a dot of liquid glue on the back of the cat's head (between where the eyes would be) and another dot about 1 in/ 2.5 cm below the first. Cut a 1-in/2.5-cm square of scrap paper. Using the glue stick, cover the paper with glue. Set the left string in the glue on the cat's head. Place the cat's head low enough so that it does not touch the words. Cover the string and glue with the square, pressing firmly. Apply the glue stick to the inside of a pennant and a dot of liquid glue on the fold. Attach to the string about 2 in/ 5 cm below the cat's head. Apply a dot of liquid glue to the center of a star and place it at the end of the string below the pennant. Repeat with another star and press the stars firmly together. Again adjust the center support string for balance.

9. Apply glue stick to the inside of the second pennant and a dot of liquid glue to the fold. Attach to the right string. Cut a ½-in/ 12-mm square of scrap paper and use it to attach the kitten to the string in the same way you attached the cat's head about 2 in/5 cm below the pennant. Apply a dot of the liquid glue to the center of a star and place it at the end of the string below the kitten. Repeat with another star and press the stars firmly together.

10. After you adjust for balance, trim any excess string across the top of the wire. You may want to move the other lengths of string, rather than only the center string, to get the balance just right. Once your

{continued}

mobile is hanging straight (or with a small amount of tilt), place a dot of liquid glue on each knot across the top of the wire. Allow to dry at least an hour before moving.

STEP 1 // STEP 2 ////////////////////////////////

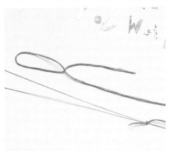  

STEP 3 ////////////////////////////// STEP 4 ////////////////////////// STEP 6 //////////////////////////////

////////////////////////////////////// STEP 7 ////////////////////////// STEP 8 //////////////////////////////

Sweet Paper Crafts

STEP 9

STEP 10

Alice in Wonderland Mobile

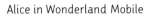

WOODLAND PARTY PUPPETS

A parade of friendly creatures out for a party, these puppets can be used to tell a story, clustered together in a bouquet, or arranged to peek out from a houseplant. These happy puppets are for children who can play responsibly with a wired object. For backing the record jacket, choose decorative papers that are sturdy but not too thick, such as those from magazines or children's books.

1. Using the glue stick, adhere your chosen backing paper to the wrong side of the record jacket. Allow to dry for about 10 minutes.

2. Download the Woodland Party Puppets templates at www.chroniclebooks.com/sweetpaper. Using the pencil, trace the deer, bear, squirrel, fox, and rabbit templates on the paper-covered jacket. Cut out the shapes with cardboard scissors. Be careful to cut inside the pencil lines so that you don't have to erase them later.

3. Trace the two crown templates, two party hat templates, and two bow tie templates on contrasting paper. Cut out with the paper scissors. Decide which creatures will wear which accessories and glue them in place with the glue stick. Allow to dry for about 10 minutes.

4. To provide added support for the puppets, cut a small rectangular piece of record jacket to fit the back of each creature. It should be as large as possible without being seen from the front. Glue in place with the glue stick.

    {continued}

Supplies

Glue stick

Paper for backing

Record jacket front or back

Woodland Party Puppets templates

Pencil

Scissors for cardboard

Contrasting paper for accessories

Scissors for paper

Wire cutters

Ruler

20-gauge straight stick floral wire

1-in/2.5-cm circle punch

Liquid glue

of the frame, tie the pieces of thread to the frame, spacing them about 3 in/7.5 cm apart. Place a tiny dot of liquid glue on each knot to keep the thread in place.

5. Download the Flowering Chandelier template at www.chroniclebooks.com/ sweetpaper. Stack three pieces of tissue paper. Use the pencil to trace the template on the top piece, then cut out through all three layers. Be careful to cut inside the pencil line so you don't have to erase it later. Separate the three layers of petals. Place a dot of liquid glue along the straight edge of one petal, in the center. This will be your bottom layer. Place a second petal on top, adhering the two together. This will be your middle layer. Apply another dot of glue in the center of the middle petal, along the straight edge, and place the last petal on top. Fold the stack gently in half, and place a small dot of glue on the top layer inside the fold. Place this glue dot on a piece of the metallic thread, very close to where the thread meets the frame. Pinch the flower around the thread until it adheres to the thread. Make more flowers in the same way and glue them to the thread, overlapping them and occasionally leaving space for leaves.

6. If you are using sewing pattern pieces for the leaves, you may need to iron the pieces on a low setting to smooth out folds and wrinkles. For each leaf, cut a piece of tissue paper about 4 by 1 in/10 cm by 2.5 cm. Fold in half lengthwise. Cut fringe in each narrow end. Apply a dot of glue to the inside of the fold. Pinch the glue-dotted leaf on the thread underneath the flower that you glued to the chandelier.

{continued}

of the frame, tie the pieces of thread to the frame, spacing them about 3 in/7.5 cm apart. Place a tiny dot of liquid glue on each knot to keep the thread in place.

5. Download the Flowering Chandelier template at www.chroniclebooks.com/sweetpaper. Stack three pieces of tissue paper. Use the pencil to trace the template on the top piece, then cut out through all three layers. Be careful to cut inside the pencil line so you don't have to erase it later. Separate the three layers of petals. Place a dot of liquid glue along the straight edge of one petal, in the center. This will be your bottom layer. Place a second petal on top, adhering the two together. This will be your middle layer. Apply another dot of glue in the center of the middle petal, along the straight edge, and place the last petal on top. Fold the stack gently in half, and place a small dot of glue on the top layer inside the fold. Place this glue dot on a piece of the metallic thread, very close to where the thread meets the frame. Pinch the flower around the thread until it adheres to the thread. Make more flowers in the same way and glue them to the thread, overlapping them and occasionally leaving space for leaves.

6. If you are using sewing pattern pieces for the leaves, you may need to iron the pieces on a low setting to smooth out folds and wrinkles. For each leaf, cut a piece of tissue paper about 4 by 1 in/10 cm by 2.5 cm. Fold in half lengthwise. Cut fringe in each narrow end. Apply a dot of glue to the inside of the fold. Pinch the glue-dotted leaf on the thread underneath the flower that you glued to the chandelier.

{continued}

Sweet Paper Crafts

FLOWERING CHANDELIER

Adding the perfect glow to any dark corner of your house, this chandelier, created from a new or used lamp shade, is encircled with clusters of pretty paper flowers and leaves. It is best made with a two-tiered shade that has a universal fitting—where the fitting for the lightbulb is in the center of the shade. You will also need a hanging lantern cord and a low-wattage bulb. If you like, you can vary the flowers by using three layers of sewing pattern tissue, three layers of colored tissue paper, or a combination of the two.

1. If your lamp shade is covered with fabric or paper, use the cardboard scissors to remove all the covering material. If necessary, eliminate any old dried glue with glue remover. You want the shade to be as clean as possible so it will take the spray paint evenly.

2. (I recommend spreading newspapers over your work area before starting this step.) Following the manufacturer's instructions and using a light hand, cover the lamp shade frame with two coats of spray paint, allowing the paint to dry between coats. After you apply the second coat, allow the frame to dry completely, at least an hour.

3. Turn the frame so the widest part is facing up. Run the cord through the center and screw in the lightbulb. Install the cup hook from the ceiling following the manufacturer's instructions, and hang the shade from the cord.

4. Using the paper scissors, cut pieces of metallic thread about 12 in/30.5 cm long (or longer or shorter depending on the size of your frame). Starting at the bottom tier

{continued}

Supplies

Two-tiered lamp shade with a universal fitting

Scissors for cardboard

Glue remover such as Goo Gone (optional)

Newspapers (optional)

Multipurpose spray paint in a coordinating color

Hanging lantern cord

Low-wattage lightbulb

20-lb/9-kg cup hook

Scissors for paper

Ruler

Silver metallic thread

Liquid glue

Flowering Chandelier template

Tissue paper for petals

Pencil

Tissue paper or sewing pattern pieces in a contrasting color for leaves

Iron (optional)

5. Using the wire cutters, cut five 9-in/23-cm pieces of floral wire. With the circle punch, punch five paper circles, one for each puppet. Dot a small amount of liquid glue on the small rectangle on the back of each creature. Place one end of a piece of wire in the glue. Using the glue stick, apply glue to a paper circle and place it on top of the liquid glue and the end of the wire. Press to secure. Allow to dry for about an hour before handling the puppets.

STEP 1 ////////////////////////////

STEP 2 ////////////////////////////

STEP 3 ////////////////////////////

////////////////////////////////////

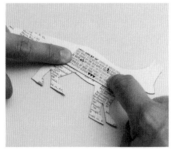

STEP 4 ////////////////////////////

STEP 5 ////////////////////////////

//

WOODLAND PARTY PUPPETS

A parade of friendly creatures out for a party, these puppets can be used to tell a story, clustered together in a bouquet, or arranged to peek out from a houseplant. These happy puppets are for children who can play responsibly with a wired object. For backing the record jacket, choose decorative papers that are sturdy but not too thick, such as those from magazines or children's books.

1. Using the glue stick, adhere your chosen backing paper to the wrong side of the record jacket. Allow to dry for about 10 minutes.

2. Download the Woodland Party Puppets templates at www.chroniclebooks.com/ sweetpaper. Using the pencil, trace the deer, bear, squirrel, fox, and rabbit templates on the paper-covered jacket. Cut out the shapes with cardboard scissors. Be careful to cut inside the pencil lines so that you don't have to erase them later.

3. Trace the two crown templates, two party hat templates, and two bow tie templates on contrasting paper. Cut out with the paper scissors. Decide which creatures will wear which accessories and glue them in place with the glue stick. Allow to dry for about 10 minutes.

4. To provide added support for the puppets, cut a small rectangular piece of record jacket to fit the back of each creature. It should be as large as possible without being seen from the front. Glue in place with the glue stick.

    {continued}

Supplies

Glue stick

Paper for backing

Record jacket front or back

Woodland Party Puppets templates

Pencil

Scissors for cardboard

Contrasting paper for accessories

Scissors for paper

Wire cutters

Ruler

20-gauge straight stick floral wire

1-in/2.5-cm circle punch

Liquid glue

Continue to cut and assemble flowers and glue them to the threads, adding leaves here and there as you like.

7. Trim any excess hanging thread. Allow the glue to dry for about an hour. Then gently spread open the petals of each flower by carefully pulling the layers up and away from each other.

8. For the top tier of the frame, repeat steps 4 to 7 to complete the chandelier.

9. Take care to keep the petals and leaves away from the lightbulb. Always use a small, low-wattage bulb and turn off the light when you leave the house.

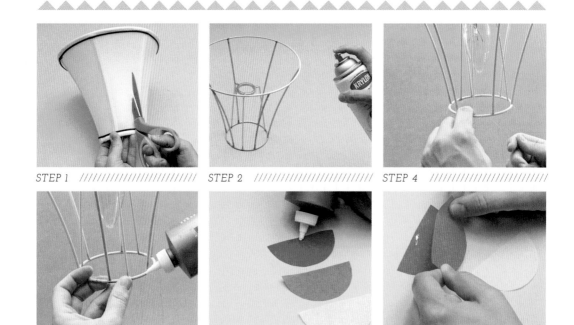

STEP 1 ////////////////////////// STEP 2 ////////////////////////// STEP 4 //////////////////////////

////////////////////////////////// STEP 5 ///

Sweet Paper Crafts

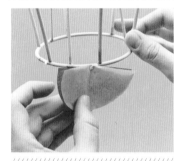
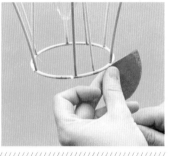

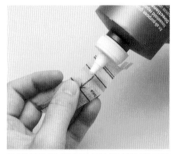

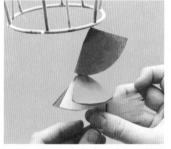

Flowering Chandelier

51

PRETTY PEOPLE CARD AND ENVELOPE

You can easily make simple collages on cards and tuck them into handmade envelopes for a special greeting. Making the collages can be lots of fun—you can cut faces from an old yearbook or clip phrases from book pages to give your characters dialogue. I like to punch little dots of confetti to include inside the card for a festive surprise, and close the envelope with a gold seal or Japanese washi tape.

1. Fold the card stock in half and use the bone folder to make the fold crisp and clean.

2. Download the Pretty People Card and Envelope templates at www.chroniclebooks .com/sweetpaper. Using the pencil and the card template, trace a card on the card stock. Cut out the card on a paper cutter to ensure clean lines and right-angled corners. Be careful to cut inside the pencil line so that you don't have to go back and erase it later.

3. Using the scissors, cut faces from the magazine pages. Trace the three body part templates on contrasting papers and cut out. Make as many body parts as you have faces. Lay the faces and body parts wrong-side down on your work surface and arrange them into a collage that will fit the front of the card. Depending on the sizes of the heads, you may need to trim the body parts for a better fit. If you like, trace the crown and party hat templates on paper and cut out. Place on the figures in the collage.

4. Using the glue stick, carefully apply glue to the back of the pieces and attach them to the front of the card in your planned

    {*continued*}

Supplies

8½ -by-11-in/21.5-by-28-cm card stock

Bone folder

Pretty People Card and Envelope templates

Pencil

Paper cutter

Scissors for paper

Magazine or yearbook pages with photos of people or animals

Papers

Glue stick

arrangement. Be careful not to smudge the glue. The more meticulous you are, the better your collage will look. Allow to dry for about 15 minutes.

5. Using the pencil, trace the envelope template on your chosen paper, then cut out. Following the fold lines on the template, fold the envelope, scoring the folds with the bone folder. Check the folds and refold if the corners don't match up the first time. Don't be afraid to trim the corners and edges if they are not lying down properly. With the glue stick, apply glue to the sides of the envelope along the folds. Slip your fingers into the envelope to be sure you didn't glue the back of the envelope to the front.

6. If your writing won't be visible because of the text or picture on the envelope, cut out an oval or a rectangle of light-colored paper and use the glue stick to attach it to the front of the envelope.

STEP 1 ///////////////////////////// STEP 2 ///////////////////////////// STEP 3 /////////////////////////////

STEP 4 /// STEP 5 /////////////////////////////

DOG TAGS

Handsome pups on leashes make for friendly greetings on gifts. To use them as ornaments on a tree, you may want to enlarge the templates by 200 percent and cut them from a heavier paper like a patterned card stock.

Supplies

Dog Tags templates

Glue stick

Sturdy magazine pages

Pencil

Scissors for paper

Ruler

String or yarn

1. Download the Dog Tags templates at www.chroniclebooks.com/sweetpaper.

2. Using the glue stick, apply glue to two magazine pages, then smoothly attach together. Allow to dry for about 10 minutes.

3. Use the pencil to trace the four dog templates on the paper. Cut out the shapes with the scissors. Be careful to cut inside the pencil lines so that you don't have to erase them later.

4. Cut four pieces of string each 8 to 10 in/ 20 to 25 cm long. Fold each string in half, bring the ends through the loop, place around the neck of a dog, and pull the ends to tighten. (If you need a space for writing a greeting, cut four shapes from paper scraps. Attach one to each tag with the glue stick.)

{continued}

STEP 2 /// STEP 3 /////////////////////////////////

STEP 4 ///

Sweet Paper Crafts

BUTTONS AND TWINE GIFT BAG

Make the packaging as lovely as the gift by creating a simple bag embellished with buttons and tied with colorful twine or yarn. This bag is beautiful whether made from vintage wrapping paper or from brown paper that comes in a roll. Unique buttons can be found in antique shops by the jarful. To make matching bags in other sizes, reduce the templates. If you are using a very delicate wrapping paper, you may want to affix butcher paper to the back of the paper with a glue stick to keep it from tearing and to make the bag sturdier. Let the glue dry for 10 minutes before cutting out the templates.

1. Download the Buttons and Twine Gift Bag templates at www.chroniclebooks.com/ sweetpaper. Tape the four bag templates together as indicated on the templates.

2. Using the pencil, trace the template on the wrapping paper twice, once with the flap and once without, as indicated on the template. Cut out with the scissors. Be careful to cut inside the pencil lines so that you don't have to erase them later. Score with the bone folder at the folds, following the dotted lines on the templates.

3. Place the bag piece with the top flap right-side down on your work surface. Place the bag piece without the top flap right-side up on the first piece, lining up the fold lines and edges. Using the glue stick, apply glue to the wrong sides of the side flaps and attach them, pressing to adhere. Be sure that the center folds on the sides are inverted. This will help the bag stand properly. Next, fold in the bottom flaps and then apply glue stick to the last flap and press to adhere. Fold the top flap over the top of the bag.

    {*continued*}

Supplies

Buttons and Twine Gift Bag templates

Tape

Pencil

Wrapping paper

Scissors for paper

Bone folder

Glue stick

Ruler

Scrap paper

Baker's twine or yarn

Yarn or sewing needle

2 lightweight buttons

Bristol board

Hole punch

4. Find the center of the top flap. Measure 1½ in/4 cm up from the bottom of the flap and mark with a dot. Measure 1½ in/4 cm down from the bottom of the top flap onto the front of the bag and mark with a dot. These are the locations for the two buttons.

5. Cut a 1-in/2.5-cm square of scrap paper and, using the glue stick, attach the square on the underside of the top flap directly under the dot for the button. This will reinforce the paper where the button will be sewn. Do the same on the front of the bag.

6. Cut a piece of baker's twine about 18 in/46 cm long. Thread the twine through the needle and tie a knot at one end. Starting from the underside of the top flap, sew a button to the bag on the dot, stitching through the button several times to secure. The last time that you stitch down through the button, tie a small knot directly behind the button. Do not clip the end, as the excess twine will be used as the tie for the button closure.

7. Thread the needle with a piece of twine about 12 in/30.5 cm long. Sew the second button to the front of the bag on the dot as done in Step 6. Knot the twine inside the bag and clip the end.

8. Trace the tag template on the Bristol board and cut out. Punch a hole in the top of the tag. Cut a 8-in/20-cm piece of baker's twine. Fold the twine in half, thread the loop through the hole in the tag, bring the ends through the loop, and pull tight.

{continued}

Sweet Paper Crafts

9. Close the bag by flipping the flap over the front and wrapping the twine in a figure eight around the buttons. Write your greeting on the tag and tie it around the figure eight.

STEP 3

STEP 4

STEP 5   STEP 6

Sweet Paper Crafts

Buttons and Twine Gift Bag

FLOWER FANCY WREATH

Crafted from exquisite crepe paper flowers, this wreath makes any doorway a pretty place to enter. Be sure to hang your wreath in a spot that is not perpetually exposed to the elements. You can also make individual flowers to string into a garland or to pin to your hair.

1. Download the Flower Fancy Wreath templates at www.chroniclebooks.com/sweetpaper.

2. Each flower has a stamen, multiple petals, and two leaves. To make a stamen, use the scissors to cut a strip of crepe paper 2 in/5 cm wide by 5 in/12 cm long. Fold the strip in half widthwise and fold in half widthwise again. Cut fringe along one side, being careful to cut only about 1½ in/4 cm into the paper. Unfold the paper so you have a 5-in/12-cm-long piece with fringe along the length.

3. Using the wire cutters, cut a 4-in/10-cm length of floral wire. Apply a small amount of liquid glue to one end of the paper on the edge without the fringe. Place one end of the floral wire on the glue and wrap the paper tightly around the wire. Apply glue to the end of the fringed paper, gently pull tight, and press the end on the wire to secure.

4. Using the pencil, trace the flower template on crepe paper, aligning the template so that the lines on the crepe paper run vertically on the template. Cut five to seven petals. Be careful to cut inside the pencil lines so you don't have to erase them later. Carefully stretch out each petal to create a more natural shape.

{continued}

Supplies

Flower Fancy Wreath templates

Scissors for paper

Ruler

Crepe paper for stamens and flowers

Wire cutters

Cloth-wrapped floral wire

Liquid glue

Pencil

Contrasting crepe paper for leaves

Floral tape

24-gauge galvanized steel wire

Fine silver wire

5. Gently pleat the bottom edge of a petal. Apply a small amount of liquid glue to the pleated edge and attach the petal to the stamen directly beneath the fringe. Continue pleating petals and attaching them around the stamen until the flower is as full as you want it to be.

6. Use the leaf template to cut two leaves from contrasting crepe paper. Apply a dab of liquid glue to the bottom of a leaf and attach it directly under the petals. Repeat with the other leaf.

7. To finish off the flower, cut a strip of crepe paper the same color as the flower about ½ in/12 mm wide by 6 in/15 cm long. Apply a small amount of glue to one end and carefully wrap it around the wire stem to cover the bottom of the petals and leaves, tightening the strip as you wrap and adding more glue as needed. Or use floral tape to cover the bottom of the petals and leaves. Bend the petals outward slightly to create a natural flower shape.

8. Repeat the process to create more flowers. Depending on the fullness of your flowers, you will need eighteen to twenty-five flowers for a 12-in/30.5-cm-diameter wreath. Allow the flowers to dry for at least an hour before attaching them to the wreath form.

9. Using the wire cutters, cut a piece of steel wire about 36 in/91 cm long. Shape the wire into a 12-in/30.5-cm-diameter circle. Tightly wrap a 4-in/10-cm piece of fine silver wire around the ends of the steel wire. Trim with the wire cutters.

Sweet Paper Crafts

10. Tightly wrap the stem of a flower around the wreath form. Attach the remaining flowers, spacing them about 1 in/2.5 cm apart. Bend the flowers as you like to make them face different directions. Wrap the wreath with floral tape to give it a neat finish, weaving the tape between the flowers and bending them slightly if necessary. Hang the wreath and adjust the flowers as needed.

STEP 2 ///

STEP 3 ///////////////////////////

///////////////////////////////////////

STEP 4 /////////////////////////

STEP 5 ///////////////////////////

{continued}

// STEP 6 ////////////////////////////////

STEP 7 // STEP 9 ////////////////////////////

STEP 10 ///

Sweet Paper Crafts

STRIPED DECOUPAGE PICTURE FRAME

This striped frame can hold a photograph or a piece of art, or can be displayed on its own. Using papers in a rainbow of colors and designs will make the frame pop off the wall. Choosing muted tones and printed pages from books will create a more subdued look. Select frames with clean lines to facilitate the decoupage process, and do not skip the sandpapering step.

1. Remove the backing and glass from the picture frame and save for later use. Sand all the surfaces of the frame with the sandpaper until the wood is smooth and free of bumps and imperfections. Wipe down with a damp rag to remove any sanding dust. Set aside to dry.

2. The widths, lengths, and quantity of the paper strips you need will depend on the size and thickness of your frame. Experiment with strips of different sizes to decide what looks best. Very thick pages will be hard to decoupage smoothly on the frame; very thin pages may tear when wet with glue. You may wish to experiment with different weights of papers before you begin. Using the paper cutter, cut strips of your chosen paper into pieces long enough to wrap around the frame from front to back. Experiment by wrapping the strips around your frame to determine how wide you want them to be and how you want to alternate the colors.

3. Lay out all the strips on your work surface in the order in which you will use them on the frame. Pour a small amount of the Mod Podge into the dish. One at a time, dip the strips into the glue and wipe off

    {continued}

Supplies

Oval wood picture frame

Medium-grade (80–120 grit) sandpaper

Clean rag

Pliable papers in a variety of colors or designs

Paper cutter

Thin liquid glue such as Mod Podge

Small dish

2 foam brushes

2 to 4 cans of equal height

Low-gloss polyurethane (optional)

any excess with a foam brush. Fit a strip of paper on the frame, and as you wrap it around the frame, press down with clean fingers to remove any air bubbles or wrinkles. Continue adding strips, overlapping them slightly, until the frame is covered.

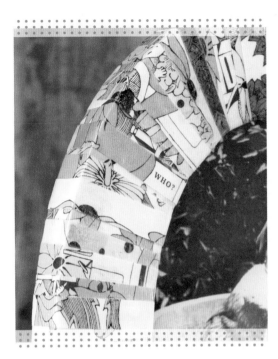

4. Arrange the cans on your work surface, set the frame on the cans, and allow to dry for 24 hours. Don't worry about glue smudges on the back of the frame where it rests on the cans.

5. Turn the frame and gently sand off any bumps on the back. If you want a matte finish, leave the frame as is or cover it with another coat of thin liquid glue and allow it to dry again for 24 hours.

6. For a shinier, more finished look, cover the face and sides of the frame with a thin coat of polyurethane using a clean foam brush. Do not overload the brush with the polyurethane. Check for drips and puddles on the surface and make sure you get a smooth finish. Place the frame on the cans and allow to dry thoroughly for at least 24 hours. Apply a second coat, check for drips, and allow to dry again. Apply as many coats as you like, letting the frame dry completely between coats. The more coats of polyurethane you apply, the more the paper edges will blend together and look almost painted onto the frame. When the frame has thoroughly dried, repeat on the back.

{*continued*}

STEP 1 /// STEP 2 ////////////////////////////////

STEP 3 ///

STEP 6 /////////////////////////////

PARTY POPPER

A popper is easier to make than you think, and one that you create is much lovelier than the mass-produced version sold at party stores. Give one to every guest, and the poppers will be the life of your party. This popper has a cracker snap—two thin strips of overlapped cardboard that, when pulled from both ends, produce a loud pop. The snaps can be purchased online. You can also omit them if you wish.

1. Using the paper scissors, cut a piece of crepe paper 12 in/30.5 cm long by 6½ in/16½ cm wide. With the cardboard scissors, cut the paper towel tube into three sections: one 5-in/12-cm piece and two 3-in/7.5-cm pieces. Lay the crepe paper on your work surface with a long side facing you. Line up the pieces of tube along the edge of the paper, placing the long piece in the middle and centering the pieces on the paper. Using a small piece of double-sided tape, affix the paper to the 5-in/12-cm tube. Holding all three pieces, roll to wrap them neatly in the paper. Affix the paper to the center of the wrapped tube with another piece of double-sided tape.

2. Insert the cracker snap into the tube so that equal lengths are sticking out the ends. If the cracker snap sticks out too far, trim each end until it's the right length. Feel the outside of the popper for the separation between the center tube and one of the shorter outer tubes. Carefully push down all around the separation and slip out the shorter tube. Cut two pieces of ribbon each 6 in/15 cm. Tie one around the paper at the end of the cracker snap where the shorter tube was removed.

{*continued*}

Supplies

. . . .

Scissors for paper

Ruler

Crepe paper

Scissors for cardboard

11-in/28-cm-long paper towel tube

Double-sided tape

11-in/28-cm cracker snap

Ribbon

Confetti

Small prizes like coins, costume jewelry, and candy

Dictionary pages

Glue stick

3. Fill the center tube of the popper from the other end with confetti and prizes. Do not overfill the tube otherwise the cracker snap may not function. Carefully push down all around the separation between the center tube and the remaining smaller outer tube, and slip out the shorter tube. Tie the remaining piece of ribbon around the paper at the end of the cracker snap. Using the paper scissors, cut fringe in the paper at each end of the popper, being careful not to cut the cracker snap.

4. Cut a piece of dictionary paper 6½ in/ 16.5 cm long by 3 in/7.5 cm wide. Using the glue stick, cover one side with glue, wrap it around the popper, and press to adhere. Allow to dry for at least 10 minutes before popping the popper.

5. To pop the popper, two people grasp both the fringe and the ends of the cracker snap and pull them simultaneously.

{continued}

Sweet Paper Crafts

STEP 1 ///

STEP 3 ///

STEP 4 ///////////////////////////////

Sweet Paper Crafts

PRANCING REINDEER ORNAMENTS

A winter-scape is not the same without reindeer dancing in the snow. A modest glint of glitter makes the ornaments stand out on a tree—perhaps reminiscent of sleigh bells in the moonlight?

1. Download the Prancing Reindeer Ornaments templates at www.chroniclebooks .com/sweetpaper. Choose two pieces of magazine pages each big enough to accommodate a reindeer template. Using the glue stick, thoroughly cover the paper with glue and glue each paper to card stock. (If pockets remain uncovered, the layers might separate after cutting.) Allow to dry for about 10 minutes. Using the pencil, trace each template on the paper-covered stock. Cut out with the scissors. You may want to use the X-ACTO knife to cut around the antlers and heads. Be careful to cut inside the pencil lines so that you don't have to erase them later.

2. Cut two pieces of embroidery floss each 8 in/20 cm long. Fold each piece in half. Apply a small dot of liquid glue to the back of each reindeer, around the shoulder area, and place the loose ends of the floss in the glue.

3. Using the punch, make two circles from paper scraps. Using the glue stick, apply glue to each circle and set on top of the liquid glue, sandwiching the floss ends in place.

{continued}

Supplies

. . . .

Prancing Reindeer Ornaments templates

Sturdy magazine pages

Glue stick

Card stock

Pencil

Scissors for paper

X-ACTO knife (optional)

Ruler

Metallic embroidery floss

Liquid glue

1-in/2.5-cm circle or medallion punch

Glitter

4. Apply a small amount of liquid glue to the edges of each reindeer in a few places, such as the nose, a couple of the hooves, and the tail. Lay down a scrap paper to catch the glitter and sprinkle the reindeer with glitter over the paper. Hang the reindeer to dry for about an hour.

STEP 1 /// STEP 2 /////////////////////////

/// STEP 3 /////////////////////////

///////////////////////////////// STEP 4 ///

PARTY-TIME PARTY HATS

Any occasion that calls for a party certainly warrants party hats—including one that you can pin in your hair. These hats look good on kids and grownups alike. Variations on the embellishments are endless and almost as fun as the party itself!

Supplies

Party-Time Party Hats templates

Pencil

Scissors for paper

Liquid glue

Ruler

Starry Crown

White butcher paper

Glue stick

Masking tape

Metallic crepe paper

Japanese washi tape (optional)

Chrysanthemum Cone Hat

White butcher paper

Glue stick

Ribbon

Crepe paper in various colors

Top Hat

Black card stock

Hot glue gun and hot glue sticks

Alligator hair clip

Newspaper (optional)

Thin liquid glue such as Mod Podge

Small dish

Foam brush

Scrap paper

Black glitter

Magazine page

1-in/2.5-cm circle or medallion punch

Paper for medallion circle

Download the Party-Time Party Hats templates at www.chroniclebooks.com/sweetpaper.

1. **To make the starry crown:** Adhere two pieces of butcher paper together using the glue stick. Allow it to dry for about 10 minutes. Attach the crown template bands to the crown base using masking tape. Using the pencil, trace the crown template on the prepared butcher paper, and cut out with the scissors.

{continued}

2. Using the liquid glue, adhere a piece of the metallic crepe paper to a piece of the butcher paper. Allow to dry for about 20 minutes. Trace the three star templates on the prepared metallic paper and cut out. Cut as many stars as you want to use on your crown. Using a light hand, attach the stars to the crown base and band with liquid glue. Adjust the band to fit the wearer and trim as necessary, leaving a 2-in/5-cm overlap. Adhere the ends of the crown band with the glue stick or washi tape. Allow to dry for about an hour before wearing.

1. ***To make the chrysanthemum cone hat:*** Adhere two pieces of butcher paper using the glue stick. Allow to dry for about 10 minutes. Trace the cone template on the prepared butcher paper and cut out. Roll into a cone. Apply liquid glue along the tab and glue in place. Cut two pieces of ribbon about 20 in/50 cm for ties. Using the liquid glue, adhere the ribbons to the outside of the hat directly across from each other.

2. Stack three colors of crepe paper. Cut a 3-in-/7.5-cm-wide strip, through all layers, long enough to go around the bottom of the hat. Fold the stacked paper lengthwise into fourths. Cut fringe nearly to the center on both long edges of the paper. Apply a very thin line of the liquid glue around the base of the hat about ½ in/12 mm from the bottom. Unfold the paper and attach one strip to the line of glue, being sure to glue the area of the strip without the fringe. Apply a line of glue to the center of the first strip and attach the second strip. Repeat with the third strip, using small dots of glue spaced about 2 in/5 cm

apart. The liquid glue will warp the crepe paper, but the flowers will cover the warped places in the next step.

3. Cut a strip of crepe paper 2 in/5 cm wide and 25 in/63.5 cm long. Starting at one end, pleat the strip widthwise to make a flower by pinching the strip of paper and applying glue here and there as you pleat to keep the folds together. Make enough flowers to attach them every 2 in/5 cm around the base of the hat (about nine flowers). Allow the flowers to dry for about 30 minutes. Clip the back of the flower to make a flat surface. Apply a dot of glue to the flat surface and press into place on the fringe, holding the flower in place a few minutes.

4. Cut a strip of crepe paper about 2 in/5 cm wide and 10 in/25 cm long. Fold length- wise into fourths. Cut fringe along one unfolded edge nearly to the opposite edge of the strip of paper. Without unfolding the fringed paper strip, pinch it along the bottom of the unfringed edge. Apply a dab of liquid glue to the inside of the hat at the peak of the cone to keep the fringe in place and push the pinched end of the fringe into the hole at the top of the hat. Allow to dry completely, about an hour. Fluff the fringe and push open the flower petals before wearing the hat.

1. **To make the top hat:** Trace the three hat templates on card stock and cut out. Shape the walls of the hat into a cylinder. Apply liquid glue to the side tab and glue to the wall, pressing firmly. Hold for about 5 min- utes. The top of the hat is wider than the bottom. Bend in the tabs at the top of the hat and apply liquid glue to the tabs.

{continued}

Adhere the top of the hat to the tabs. Next, bend out the tabs on the bottom of the hat and apply liquid glue to the undersides. Attach the tabs to the brim. Allow to dry for about 10 minutes.

2. Using the hot glue gun, attach the hair clip to the underside of the hat. Allow to dry for about 5 minutes.

3. (I recommend covering your work surface with newspaper before starting this step.) Pour the thin liquid glue into a small dish. Place the hat upright, and apply a thin layer of thin liquid glue with the foam brush. Working over a scrap paper, cover the hat with glitter. Shake off the excess onto the scrap paper. Check for places that need more glitter, brush with glue, and sprinkle on more glitter. Allow to dry for about an hour.

4. Trace the feather template on the magazine paper and cut out. Attach the feather to the hat at the quill with liquid glue, and hold in place to dry for about 5 minutes. Punch out a circle from your chosen paper. Using the glue stick and a dot of liquid glue, glue it to the base of the feather. Allow to dry for about 30 minutes before wearing.

STARRY CROWN STEP 2 //

CHRYSANTHEMUM CONE HAT STEP 1 //

STEP 2 //

/// STEP 3 ///////////////////////////

{continued}

STEP 4 //

TOP HAT STEP 1 //

Sweet Paper Crafts

STEP 2 ///////////////////////// STEP 3 ///////////////////////// STEP 4 /////////////////////////

STREAMER AND FLAG STRAWS

Slip these straws into fancy drinks or wave them like flags at a party. You can use a variety of papers other than those listed here, and if you like, you can add extra ribbons. The possibilities for adorning paper straws are endless. Tall straws are best for waving and for soda fountain drinks; for shorter glasses, snip the straws to size.

Download the Streamer and Flag Straws templates at www.chroniclebooks.com/sweetpaper.

1. **To make the streamer straw:** Using the scissors, cut six strips of dictionary paper each 1/4 in/6 mm wide by 6 in/15 cm long. Stack the strips. Starting at the center of the stack, gently but tightly twist the stack once. Place a dot of liquid glue in the center of the twist and attach to a straw about 2 in/5 cm from the top. Wrap the stack around the straw, cross the ends, and apply a dot of glue underneath the crossed area. Place tiny dots of glue under each layer of paper to keep the tassel twist in place.

2. Layer four pieces of tissue paper and trace the square pouf template on to the top layer with your pencil. Cut the squares out through all four layers of tissue, being careful to cut inside the lines so that you won't have to erase pencil marks later. Accordion fold the stack of tissue squares. Cut a 4-in/10-cm piece of thread and tie the folded tissue at the center. Gently separate each layer of tissue paper to create a pouf. Trim the thread ends close to the knot. Apply a small dot of liquid glue to the back of the pouf and attach it to the straw just above the center of the tassel twist.

{continued}

Supplies
....

Streamer and Flag Straws templates

Scissors for paper

Ruler

Non-toxic liquid glue

2 paper drinking straws

Pencil

Streamer Straw

Thin dictionary paper

Tissue paper

Thread in coordinating color

Flag Straw

Paper for flags

Glue stick

Fine ribbon or rickrack in 2 colors

1. **To make the flag straw:** Lightly fold a piece of paper in half. Line up the large flag template along the fold as noted on the template and use the pencil to trace the flag onto the paper. Cut out the flag, leaving the fold intact. Be careful to cut inside the pencil lines so that you don't have to erase them later. Open up the folded flag and apply glue stick all over the inside of the flag. Apply a thin line of liquid glue to the crease of the fold and place the straw on the liquid glue line, about 2 in/5 cm from the top of the straw. Fold the flag shut around the straw and press to adhere the edges together.

2. Cut a 6-in/15-cm length of ribbon of each color. Place a ribbon on your work surface and apply a dot of glue in the center of the length of one piece of ribbon. Find the center of the second piece of ribbon and press it onto the glue on the first ribbon, adhering the two together. Place a dot of glue in the center of the length of the top ribbon. Press the glued ribbons onto the straw directly below the flag. Wrap the ends of the ribbons around the straw. Wait 10 minutes for the glue to dry and then tie a small knot where the ribbons are joined together.

3. Trace the small flag template on to folded paper, following fold lines. Cut out with the scissors. Open up the flag and apply glue stick to the inside. Apply a thin line of liquid glue to the fold and place one of the ribbons in the glue. Fold the flag closed and press to adhere. Trim the ribbons if you like.

STREAMER STRAW STEP 1 //

// STEP 2 ///

///

// FLAG STRAW STEP 1 //

{continued}

Streamer and Flag Straws

91

//

// STEP 3 ///

CELEBRATION CAKE BANNER

Dresden gold foil paper letters are a classic crafting embellishment. String these letters together on shiny metallic gold thread and spell a special message for someone you're celebrating. Plan out the letters needed in advance and order them from an online source (I get mine from eBay). Use square foam blocks found in the floral department of craft stores to support your banner while you're working on it. When you're done, place the banner on top of a cake for an unexpected personal touch.

1. Pierce each skewer into a foam block. Space the blocks at the distance you intend to hang your banner on a cake.

2. Using the scissors, cut a length of metallic thread for the strand of letters, allowing extra thread for tying the ends. Lay the thread on your work surface. Arrange the letters on the thread to spell your message and check for spacing to make the words readable.

3. Turn the letters right-side down and apply a minuscule drop of glue to the backs of the letters toward the top. Place the thread in the glue. The glue will dry clear, and if you do not use too much, you won't even see it on the back of the banner. Allow to dry for about an hour.

4. Tie the ends of each strand to the skewers, being careful to keep the letters from hanging too low. Secure each knot with a tiny drop of liquid glue. Place the skewers in your cake!

{continued}

Supplies

2 wood skewers

Two 2-in/5-cm cubed foam blocks

Scissors for paper

Metallic gold thread

Dresden gold foil paper letters

Liquid glue

STEP 1 ////////////////////////////////

STEP 2 ////////////////////////////////

STEP 3 ////////////////////////////////

STEP 4 ////////////////////////////////

//

//

STAR CLUSTER GARLAND

Perfect stars are strung together for festooning a doorway, a mantel, or any spot that needs to twinkle. Using a sturdy magazine or a similar weight paper will help the stars keep their shape. If you like, you can apply glitter here and there to add some extra sparkle.

Supplies

Star Cluster Garland templates

Pencil

Sturdy paper

Scissors for paper

Glue stick

Liquid glue

Ruler

Strong thread

Yarn needle

1. Download the Star Cluster Garland templates at www.chroniclebooks.com/sweetpaper. For each three-dimensional star, you will need four stars of the same size. For a 6-ft/2-m garland that uses all three sizes of stars, you will need to make at least six three-dimensional stars of each size. This means you need to cut twenty-four stars from each template.

2. Using the pencil, trace the star templates onto paper. Cut out with the scissors. Irregular stars will be difficult to fit together, so cut the stars as precisely as you can. Be careful to cut inside the pencil lines so that you don't have to erase them later.

3. Holding a star so that one of the points is at the top, cut a slit between the bottom two points (labeled "A" and "B" on the templates) up into the center of the star. Using the glue stick, apply glue to cover the "A" point of the star. Attach this point to the *underside* of the "B" point of the star. Press together. This conjoined point is now called point "AB." The star now has four points, and the center is inverted. Repeat this step with all of the stars.

{*continued*}

Sweet Paper Crafts

4. Pair two four-point inverted stars of the same size. On one of the stars, apply glue stick to the back (not the inverted side) of point "AB." Take the other star and, matching the "AB" points on each star, attach the two "AB" points together. Press to adhere. This conjoined point is now called the "joined AB" point. Repeat this step with the remaining stars. Now each pair is half of a three-dimensional star.

5. Pair two half three-dimensional stars of the same size. Find the "joined AB" point on one half star and hold the point between the thumb and index finger of one hand. Apply liquid glue to the back side of the star. Holding the other half star in the same way, firmly press the centers together on the glue and hold for about a minute. Repeat to form the remaining three-dimensional stars.

6. Cut a 6-ft/2-m length of thread and thread the needle. Line up your stars in the order in which you want them to appear on the garland. Push the needle through the centers of the stars and thread them together. Tie loops on the ends of the thread and hang the garland.

Sweet Paper Crafts

STEP 3 //

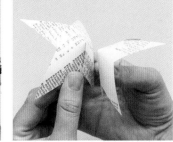

// STEP 4 ///

STEP 5 /// STEP 6 //////////////////////////////

//

PAPER SHIP PACKAGE TOPPER

Sail into a party carrying a package with a boat cresting waves of paper cones. Just make sure that the gift inside is as stunning as the topper! For the base, choose a vintage record jacket and papers with colors that coordinate well.

1. Download the Paper Ship Package Topper templates at www.chroniclebooks.com/ sweetpaper. Using the pencil, trace the star base template and the tag template on the record jacket. Cut them out with the cardboard scissors. Be careful to cut inside the pencil lines so that you don't have to erase them later. Punch a hole at the narrow end of the tag. Cut a 10-in/25-cm piece of string with the paper scissors. Fold in half to make a loop, thread the loop into the hole in the tag, bring the ends through the loop, and tighten.

2. Cut two or three 6-in/15-cm pieces of velvet ribbon. Fold each piece in half to form a loop. Using the liquid glue, glue the loops and tag strings in a cluster slightly off center on the star base. Press to secure. Allow to dry for about 15 minutes.

3. Trace the leaf pattern on your chosen paper and cut out two or three leaves. Apply liquid glue to one end of each leaf and place on the star base so that it extends slightly off the star. Press to secure. Repeat with the remaining leaves, grouping them as you like.

{continued}

Supplies

Paper Ship Package Topper templates

Pencil

Record jacket front or back

Scissors for cardboard

Hole punch

Ruler

String or twine

Scissors for paper

Velvet ribbon

Liquid glue

Papers

Scallop scissors

Glue stick

Wire cutters

20-gauge straight stick floral wire

Sturdy needle

Toothpick

Yes! Paste

Double-sided tape

4. Trace the circle template on your chosen paper. You will need fourteen to eighteen circles. Cut out with the scallop scissors. Roll up each circle to form a cone. Apply a small amount of liquid glue where the paper overlaps. Repeat to make the remaining cones.

5. Make a circle of cones on the star base, arranging the narrow ends toward the center and covering the ends of the ribbon and leaves. Glue the cones to the base with liquid glue. Allow to dry for about 30 minutes.

6. Glue two pieces of paper together with the glue stick for the boat pieces. Allow to dry for about 10 minutes. Trace the boat, sail, and flag templates on the layered paper and cut out with the paper scissors. Fold the boat in half and glue the ends together with glue stick, pinching them to secure.

7. Using wire cutters, cut a 6-in/15-cm piece of floral wire. Using the needle, pierce holes in the sail, flag, and boat as indicated on the templates. Thread the wire through the holes in the flag and then the holes in the sail. Insert into the hole in the boat. You should have 1 to 2 in/ 2.5 to 5 cm of wire at the bottom. Bend the end of the wire under the boat to make an L shape. Using the toothpick, apply a small amount of Yes! Paste to the L. Carefully maneuver the end of the wire in the center of the circle of cones on the star base. If the wire is too long, slide the boat and flags down the wire and trim the excess

wire at the top. Hold the wire in place for about 5 minutes. You may need to attach additional paper cones underneath the boat to make the boat look like it's floating on the cones. Apply a small amount of liquid glue to the last cones and glue into place as necessary. The bottom of the boat should be resting on the cones.

8. Allow to dry for about an hour. Use double-sided tape on the bottom of the star base to attach the topper to a package.

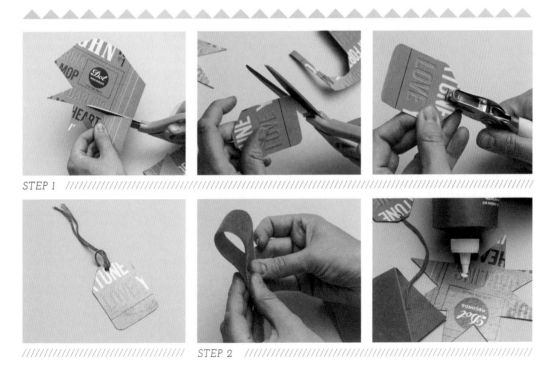

STEP 1

STEP 2

{continued}

Paper Ship Package Topper

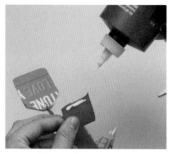  

/////////////////////////////// STEP 3 /////////////////////////// STEP 4 ///////////////////////////

///

STEP 5 /////////////////////// STEP 6 ///

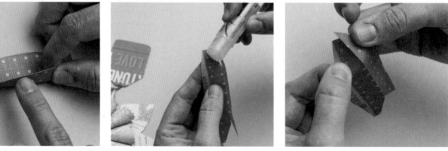

///

Sweet Paper Crafts

//

///

///

SQUARES AND DIAMONDS MOBILE

Catching a breeze and taking a spin, this mobile boasts a cluster of geometric shapes. The mobile can be made with any number of shapes grouped together: ovals, triangles, birds, or stars. Using old record jackets brings a personal, handcrafted feel.

Supplies

Squares and Diamonds Mobile templates

Record jacket front or back

Pencil

Scissors for cardboard

Paper liner from record jacket

Scissors for paper

Sturdy needle

Ruler

Silver metallic thread

Liquid glue

Glue stick

Papers for squares and diamonds

1. Download the Squares and Diamonds Mobile templates at www.chroniclebooks.com/sweetpaper.

2. Decide if you want to use the front or back of the record jacket. The design will show on the top of the mobile base, so make sure that it coordinates with the rest of your papers. Using the pencil, trace the diamond base template on the record jacket and cut out with the cardboard scissors. Be careful to cut inside the pencil line so that you don't have to erase it later. All of the mobile shapes will hang from this base.

3. Using the record-jacket diamond as a template, trace the same shape on one layer of the paper liner. Cut out with the paper scissors.

4. Find the center of the record-jacket diamond base, and pierce a hole through it with the needle. Align the base with the record-liner diamond and pierce a hole in the center. Cut a 14-in/35.5-cm piece of silver thread. Working from underneath the record-jacket base, push an end of the thread through the hole in the center. Then pass it back through the hole, leaving a 6-in/15-cm loop at the top for hanging the mobile. Place a small dot of liquid glue on the ends of the thread at the center hole to adhere the threads to the jacket.

    {continued}

5. Pierce a hole at each of the four points of the liner diamond only. Cut five pieces of silver thread, each about 25 in/ 63.5 cm long. Thread an end of each piece through one of the holes in the paper-liner diamond. Use liquid glue to secure each end to the liner.

6. Using the glue stick, apply glue thoroughly but smoothly to the wrong side of the record-jacket diamond, where the ends of the hanging loops are glued. Attach the side of the paper-liner diamond with the glued thread ends to the wrong side of the record-jacket diamond, aligning the edges. The ends of all the threads are now sandwiched between the two pieces. The top of the base is the record-jacket piece with the thread loop. The five long threads hang down from the bottom of the base. Allow the base to dry thoroughly, at least an hour.

7. Use the pencil to trace the three diamond templates and three square templates on your chosen paper. Each of the five strings will need about ten to twelve shapes, depending on how you want to space them. Cut out all the shapes.

8. Hang the mobile base from the loop. Arrange pairs of matching shapes on your work surface and decide how you want to place them on the threads. Using the glue stick, coat one side of each shape with glue. Glue the shapes to one of the hanging threads, sandwiching the thread between them. Repeat until you have filled all the threads. Trim any excess thread at the ends.

Sweet Paper Crafts

9. If the mobile is imbalanced, cut small geometric shapes from the record-jacket scraps. Coat a shape with liquid glue and attach it to the top of the base near the hanging loop. Attach a few more pieces if necessary until the mobile hangs properly. A slight tilt will cause the mobile to catch a breeze and turn more gracefully than if the base hangs flat.

10. Allow the mobile to dry overnight. Check the balance again and make any adjustments. When the mobile balances well for at least 24 hours, it's done!

STEP 4 //

// STEP 5 ///

{continued}

////////////////////////////////// STEP 6 ///

STEP 7 ///////////////////////////////// STEP 8 ///

////////////////////////////////// STEP 9 ///

//////////////////////////////////

Sweet Paper Crafts

BIRD-IN-FLIGHT PLACE SETTING

With this lovely name card, a bird looks as if it has just landed daintily to tell your guest where to sit. Honeycomb paper is available online in a wide range of colors. When you buy it in sheets, you can make lots of paper balls of any dimension, even the tiniest sizes.

1. Download the Bird-in-Flight Place Setting templates at www.chroniclebooks.com/sweetpaper. Using the pencil, trace the card template on card stock. Cut out using the scissors. Fold the card in half and score with the bone folder.

2. Trace the half-circle honeycomb template on the honeycomb paper, making sure that the lines of the paper are perpendicular to the straight side of the template. Cut out with the scissors. Using the glue stick, apply glue to each side of the half circle. Line up the straight edge of the half circle with the folded edge of the card and press to adhere. Open the half circle to form a ball, and attach it to the other side of the card so that it grasps the card. Press to adhere.

3. Trace the bird template on two layers of lightweight paper. Carefully cut out so that you have two identical birds. Be careful to cut inside the pencil line so that you don't have to erase it later. Using the glue stick, apply glue to the beak, head, and body of one bird, but not to the wings and tail feathers. Place the other bird on the glue and press firmly all around the bird. Gently bend open the wings and tail feathers.

   {*continued*}

Supplies

Bird-in-Flight Place Setting templates

Pencil

Card stock

Scissors for paper

Bone folder

Honeycomb paper

Glue stick

Lightweight paper for bird

Liquid glue

4. Apply a thin line of liquid glue to the bottom curve of the bird's body and gently place the bird on top of the honeycomb ball, slightly off center, so that the bird looks as if it has just come in for a landing. Hold in place for a few minutes, then allow to dry thoroughly for about an hour.

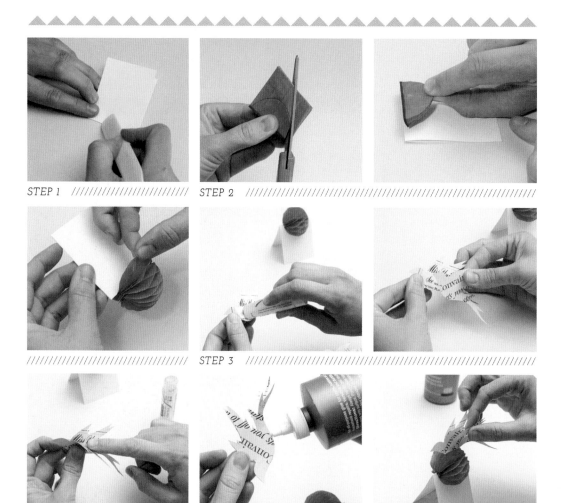

STEP 1 //////////////////////////////

STEP 2 //

//////////////////////////////////////

STEP 3 //

//////////////////////////////////////

STEP 4 //

Sweet Paper Crafts

GENTLE RABBIT TAXIDERMY

Oh-so-handsome and friendly, this wise rabbit will cozy up any space. Sculpting a creature out of boxes, newspaper, and tape may seem a challenging feat, but with a little patience and confidence, you will soon be whipping up a hutch full of bunnies.

1. Download the Gentle Rabbit Taxidermy templates at www.chroniclebooks.com/ sweetpaper. Open the cereal boxes and lay them flat. Using the pencil, trace the rabbit templates on the boxes. Cut out with the scissors. Using the templates as your guide, label the box pieces so that you know the names of the pieces and where they connect to each other.

2. Follow the labels on the pieces to assemble the rabbit. Using the masking tape, attach the SIDES OF HEAD to the top of the CENTER HEAD piece.

3. Tape the JOWLS AND CHIN piece under the sides of the head. Bend in the sides of the chin piece and tuck into the head. Stuff the head with a few strips of wadded newspaper.

4. Attach the BACK piece to the joined head pieces with the tape. Tuck the top of the CHEST piece into the head and affix with tape. Tape the bottom and one side of the CHEST piece to the bottom and one side of the BACK piece. Stuff the CHEST piece with newspaper and tape the chest closed. Cover the head and body of the rabbit with masking tape to stiffen the figure and make it smooth and sturdy.

{*continued*}

Supplies

....

Gentle Rabbit Taxidermy templates

2 cereal boxes

Pencil

Scissors for cardboard

Masking tape

Newspaper

Wire cutters

Ruler

20-gauge straight stick floral wire

Liquid glue

Glitter

Needle

Papers

Thin liquid glue such as Mod Podge

Small dish

2 foam brushes

Semi-gloss polyurethane (optional)

5. Position the EARS on the head, leaving a small space between them. Use masking tape to attach the EARS to the head and then cover them entirely with masking tape, making sure to retain the shape of the EARS.

6. The rabbit may need more definition, depending on how much masking tape you applied. Look at him from all sides to determine where he is uneven. Using small wads of newspaper and masking tape, fill out the rabbit along the outer edges of the ears, across the chest, and in the cheek area.

7. Using the wire cutters, cut a 6-in/15-cm piece of floral wire and twist to form a loop. Push the ends of the loop into the back of the neck for hanging. Secure with masking tape.

8. For whiskers, cut six pieces of wire, each about 4 in/10 cm long. Dip 2 in/5 cm of each wire into liquid glue. Roll the glued area of each wire in glitter poured on to a scrap paper. Allow to dry for about an hour. Mark the spots on the nose where you want the whiskers to go, and pierce holes in the nose with the needle. Squirt a little liquid glue on the holes and push the ends of the wires without the glitter into the holes. Secure the base of each whisker with masking tape. Allow to dry for another hour.

9. Shred paper into narrow strips of various lengths. Pour the thin liquid glue into the dish. Immerse a strip of paper in the glue. Use a foam brush to wipe off any excess.

Sweet Paper Crafts

Apply the glue-covered strip to the rabbit, being careful to smooth out the wrinkles as you go. Cover one side of the rabbit with strips and allow to dry for about an hour. Repeat the process to cover the back of the rabbit. Let dry for another hour.

10. Coat the rabbit all over with the thin liquid glue for a matte finish. If you want a shiny finish, cover with a layer of polyurethane, using a separate foam brush.

11. Hang him up!

STEP 1 ////////////////////////

STEP 2 //

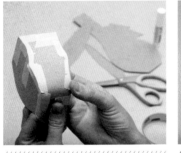

//

STEP 3 //

{continued}

Gentle Rabbit Taxidermy

STEP 4

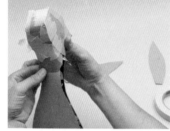

STEP 5

STEP 6

Sweet Paper Crafts

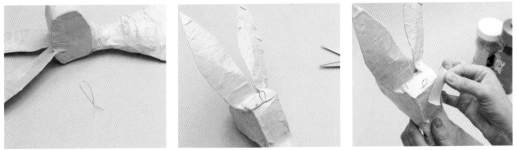

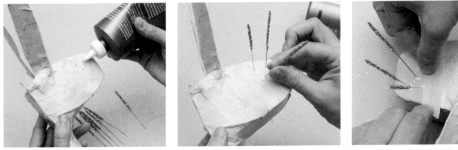

//

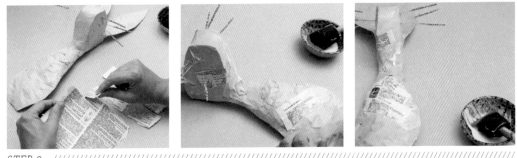

STEP 9 //

GALLOPING CUPCAKE TOPPERS

These lively horses galloping across a landscape of frosting will be the perfect finishing touch to your cupcakes. Using long toothpicks, available online, will keep their hooves clean. For an extra flourish, I like to sprinkle matching homemade confetti over the tabletop.

Supplies

Galloping Cupcake Toppers templates

Pencil

Magazine or book pages for horses

Scissors for paper

Small multiple-hole punch

Papers for confetti

Glue stick

Three 4 1/2-in/11-cm wood toothpicks or skewers

Liquid glue

1. Download the Galloping Cupcake Toppers templates at www.chroniclebooks.com/sweetpaper. Using the pencil, trace the three horse templates on two layers of your chosen paper. Carefully cut out with the scissors so that each horse has two identical pieces. Be careful to cut inside the pencil lines so that you don't have to erase them later.

2. With the multiple-hole punch, make a pile of confetti. Using the glue stick, attach confetti to both the back and the front of each horse to give it a speckled appearance.

3. Decide where and how you want to mount each horse on a toothpick. Working with matching pairs of horses, cover the wrong sides with glue stick. Add a few tiny drops of liquid glue to the center of one piece and set a toothpick in the glue with one end extending about 1 in/2.5 cm above the top of the horse. Cover with the second piece, aligning the two pieces and sandwiching the toothpick. Be sure to smooth the layers together. Repeat to glue the remaining horse pieces and toothpicks. Allow to dry for about an hour.

{*continued*}

STEP 1 //

STEP 2 //////////////////////////////////

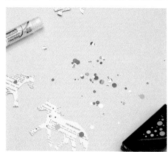

//////////////////////////////////// STEP 3 ///

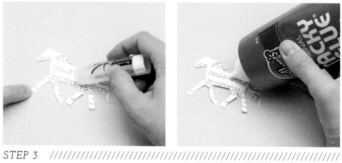

///

LEAFY LEAF HEADBAND

▼▼▼▼▼

Crown your crown with a pretty headband and leaves aplenty. Using fine spool wire to make the stems will let you arrange the leaves as you like them. For a more daring headband, enlarge the leaf templates by 300 percent and bend the wires so that the leaves perch majestically on your head. Plain headbands can be found in any craft supply store.

1. Download the Leafy Leaf Headband templates from www.chroniclebooks.com/sweetpaper. Using the pencil, trace the three leaf templates on your chosen paper. You will need about forty leaves, depending on the size of your headband. Place another piece of paper under the paper with the tracings. Cut out the leaves through both layers so that each leaf has a matching back. Be careful to cut inside the pencil lines so that you don't have to erase them later. Keep the leaf pairs together.

2. With wire cutters, cut a 4-in/10-cm length of wire for each leaf. Working with pairs of leaves, apply a small amount of liquid glue to a back leaf from the center down to the bottom. Use a light hand with the glue, as too much will warp the paper. Place one end of a wire in the glue. Using the glue stick, apply glue to the top leaf and place it on the back leaf, sandwiching the wire between the leaves. Repeat to assemble the remaining leaves and stems. Allow to dry for about an hour.

{continued}

Supplies
. . . .

Leafy Leaf Headband templates

Pencil

Papers

Scissors for paper

Wire cutters

Ruler

Fine silver wire

Liquid glue

Glue stick

Plastic or metal headband

Crepe paper

3. Try on your headband and decide where you want to attach the leaves. You don't want to place them where the headband sits behind your ears. Wrap the end of a wire stem securely around the spot where you want the leaves to start. You will cover these wires with crepe paper later, so they need to be neat to keep them from being bumpy underneath the crepe paper. After wrapping the stems on the headband, trim the end of the wire with the wire cutters. Add the next leaf so that it is going in the same direction as the first. Be sure to place it close to the first leaf so that they overlap slightly when lying on the headband. Wrap the wire neatly and trim the excess. Repeat to attach the remaining leaves.

4. Cut a ½-in-/12-mm-wide strip of single layer crepe paper that is long enough to wrap around the headband. Attach one end to the headband with a dot of liquid glue, and wrap the strip around the headband, covering all the wires, bending the leaves back and forth as needed, and adding a dot of glue here and there. Allow to dry for about an hour before bending the leaves into position. Try on the headband and bend the leaves up and out to your liking.

{*continued*}

STEP 1 ///////////////////////// STEP 2 //

STEP 3 /// STEP 4 ////////////////////////

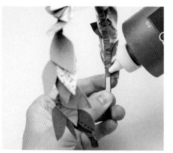

//

RESOURCES

Keeping a stash of supplies makes crafting enjoyable at any time. Look for tools and special papers at independent art supply and craft stores as well as thrift shops and yard sales. Online and chain stores are sometimes the best places to find exactly what you need. Here's a list of my favorite resources.

ART SUPPLIES

Michaels

www.michaels.com

For a one-stop supply trip, Michaels has almost everything you need to get started. It's a great resource for basic supplies like quality drawing paper and paints, paper punches, and floral wire. Some specialty items like alligator hair clips and brooch pins can also be found here.

Scotch

www.scotchbrand.com

When it comes to wrinkle-free, clear glue sticks and double-sided tape, Scotch makes my favorites. Supermarkets and craft stores carry Scotch adhesives.

Westcott

www.westcottbrand.com

Sharp, sturdy scissors with good grips are a must when working with paper. Westcott scissors can be found in most craft stores or online.

SPECIALTY PAPERS

32° North

www.vintage-ornaments.com

The folks at 32° North offer beautiful German glass glitter, a fun collection of Dresden foil trims, and a rainbow of honeycomb paper. An added bonus: The company ships your order quickly.

Nashville Wraps

www.nashvillewraps.com

I always buy tissue paper from Nashville Wraps. The paper is high quality and beautiful and comes in several sizes and colors.

Paper Source

www.paper-source.com

If you're looking for the perfect gift boxes, Paper Source has a great selection, as well as beautiful Japanese papers, spools of sparkly tinsel, and handy tools like bone folders.

ULINE

www.uline.com

I like to buy big rolls of butcher paper and rolls of masking tape from ULINE, which often ships the day it receives your order.

THREADS, YARN, AND WIRES

The Bakers Twine

www.thebakerstwine.com

The Bakers Twine offers lots of colors and spool sizes, letting you stock up so that you have a variety on hand.

Jo-Ann Fabric and Craft Stores

www.joann.com

Miles of pretty ribbon, every size of sewing needle imaginable, skeins of embroidery floss, and several colors of metallic thread are all available at JoAnn stores.

SPECIAL SUPPLIES

eBay

www.ebay.com

Old books, antique maps, vintage wrapping paper, ribbon, and Dresden foil letters—these items and more can be purchased from sellers around the world.

Olde English Crackers

www.oldenglishcrackers.com

Cracker snaps for making party poppers come in several lengths and various quantities. They are not always available year-round, so stock up during the holidays.

Oriental Trading

www.orientaltrading.com

Party poppers aren't complete without trinkets to hide inside. When you can't find them locally, check Oriental Trading for a wealth of perfect little surprises.

{continued}

Paper Lantern Store

www.paperlanternstore.com

This online store carries cord kits in multiple sizes and lightbulbs of various wattages for hanging lanterns.

Pick On Us

www.pickonus.com

Long toothpicks and skewers with carved or decorative tops can be purchased in bulk from Pick On Us. Though you have to buy a large quantity, the quality is great. And most likely you will only have to purchase a bulk order once!

PrettyTape

www.etsy.com/shop/prettytape

This is my favorite Etsy shop for buying Japanese washi tape and other decorative tapes in a seemingly infinite supply of pretty colors and patterns.

INDEX

ACKNOWLEDGMENTS

I 'm so thankful for the opportunity to collaborate on this book with a wonderful team of creative people. *Sweet Paper Crafts* wouldn't have been possible without all of you. Many kind thanks to my brilliant team at Chronicle: my editors, Laura Lee Mattingly, Claire Fletcher, Marie Oishi, and Judith Dunham; my talented designer, Jennifer Tolo Pierce; my production coordinator, Steve Kim; and my publicist, Lorraine Woodcheke. Thanks to all of you for working tirelessly and making this book happen! To Barb Blair of Knack Studios for believing in my book and in my work. To Annie Koelle for loving butterflies as much as I do and partnering with me on Etsy in the early days. To Chris Koelle for your fantastic way with hand lettering. To Erin Godbey for your beautiful (and delicious) cake baking and decorating skills. To Lily Wikoff for your ingenious styling and collection of pretty things. To my four beautiful children who ate lots of peanut butter sandwiches so that I could work on this project. And, especially, to my wonderful and handsome husband Aaron Greene for your unending support and encouragement and your beautiful photography that makes my work shine.